MONTHS

by Robin Nelson

first step nonfiction

ᐸ Lerner Publications Company · Minneapolis

April

Sunday	Monday	Tuesday	Wednesday	Thursday	Friday	Saturday
		1	2	3	4	5
6	7	8	9	10	11 No School!	12
13	14 No School!	15	16	17	18	19
20	21	22 Happy Birthday	23	24	25	26
27	28	29	30			

A **calendar** keeps track of **days, weeks,** and **months.**

There are 12 months in a **year.**

A month has between 28
and 31 days.

January is the start of a brand-new year.

February is the shortest month.

In March, spring is coming.

April is rainy.

In May, flowers are blooming.

Summer begins in June.

In July, we have picnics.

We go swimming to keep
cool in August.

In September, school begins.

Leaves fall in October.

In November, days get
colder.

We celebrate holidays in December.

Each month of the year
is special.

In what month were you born?

You can make a bar graph to show which month the kids in your class were born in. Look at the bar graph on the right for one class. You can find which month has the most birthdays. Which month has the least birthdays? Which months have the same number of birthdays?

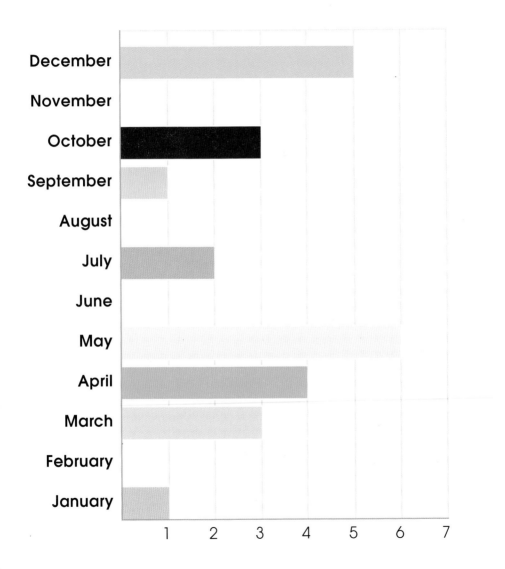

Fun Month Facts

 January is National Soup Month.

 February is National Snack Food Month.

 March is National Noodle and Peanut Month.

 April is National Frog Month.

 May is National Hamburger Month.

 June is Zoo and Aquarium Month.

July is National Hot Dog Month.

 August is National Inventor's Month.

 September is National Honey Month.

 October is National Popcorn Poppin' Month.

 November is Peanut Butter Lovers' Month.

 December is Write to a Friend Month.

Glossary

 calendar – keeps track of days, weeks, and months

 day – the time from one morning to the next morning. A day is 24 hours.

 month – a part of the year. There are 12 months in a year.

 week – an amount of time. There are 7 days in a week.

 year – an amount of time. There are 12 months in a year.

Index

The photographs in this book are reproduced through the courtesy of: © Todd Strand/Independent Picture Service, front cover, pp. 2, 3, 4, 22 (all); © John Vann/Photo Network, p. 5; © Jeff Greenberg/Visuals Unlimited, p. 6; © Bill Beaty/Visuals Unlimited, p. 7; © Trip/M. Garrett, p. 8; © Trip/M. Stevenson, p. 9; © Esbin-Anderson/Photo Network, pp. 10, 16; © Ehlers/Photo Network, pp. 11, 15; © Cynthia Salter/Photo Network, p. 12; © Tom, Dee Ann McCarthy/Photo Network, p. 13; © John D. Cunningham/Visuals Unlimited, p. 14; © Myrleen Ferguson Cate/Photo Network, p. 17.

Lerner Publications Company
A division of Lerner Publishing Group
241 First Avenue North
Minneapolis, MN 55401 U.S.A.

Website address: www.lernerbooks.com

Library of Congress Cataloging-in-Publication Data

Nelson, Robin, 1971–
    Months / by Robin Nelson.
        p.   cm. — (First step nonfiction)
    Includes index.
    ISBN: 0–8225–0179–1 (lib. bdg. : alk. paper)
    1. Calendar—Juvenile literature. 2. Months—Juvenile literature.
  [1. Months. 2. Calendar.] I. Title. II. Series.
  CE13.N45 2002
  529'.2—dc21   2001002203

Manufactured in the United States of America
3 4 5 6 7 8 – DP – 09 08 07 06 05 04